A Pocket Guide to the Command Line

Andy Stubbs

invisibleloop
Pocket Books

For Jane, Oscar and Harry

Contents

Chapter 1

About

"A Pocket Guide to the Command Line" is your essential companion for navigating the rich landscape of command-line tools. Compact yet comprehensive, this book caters to beginners, intermediates, and experts, demystifying the command line and transforming it into an accessible and powerful ally.

From the basic principles of operating systems to the nuanced techniques of networking and scripting, each chapter builds upon the last, offering a clear and cohesive learning path. Insights from the author's experience, including the valuable resources found at 24hoursintheterminal.com, bring concepts to life, while step-by-step guides ensure practical application.

Special features include in-depth explorations of text editors, customisation strategies, and an appendix filled with valuable shortcuts and troubleshooting advice. Whether you're an aspiring developer, an IT professional, or a tech hobbyist, "A Pocket Guide to the Command Line" is the key to unlocking the true power of the command line.

Take it with you on your journey through the world of technology and discover the art and craft of command line mastery, all within the convenient reach of your pocket.

About the Author

Andy, a seasoned software engineer, boasts an illustrious career spanning over 24 years in web and mobile development. A testament to perseverance and passion, much of his expertise is self-acquired. Driven by an innate desire to share and educate, Andy has an expansive portfolio encompassing websites, mobile applications, desktop software, and command-line scripts crafted to enhance productivity. Through every line of code and keystroke, he embodies the essence of continuous learning and the joy of sharing knowledge.

Chapter 2

Introduction

Importance of the Command Line

The command line, often considered the heart of an operating system, is more than just a relic of the early computing era. It provides a powerful interface for performing tasks, automation, and managing systems. While graphical interfaces are more intuitive, they often lack the depth and flexibility of the command line.

Example: You want to rename hundreds of files in a directory, changing the extension from `.txt` to `.md`. Using a GUI for this task would be tedious and time-consuming. With the command line, a single command can accomplish this task in seconds:

```
rename 's/\.txt$/.md/' *.txt
```

Code explanation: This command uses the `rename` utility to replace the .txt extension with .md for every file in the directory that ends with .txt.

Basics of Operating Systems: Unix/Linux, macOS, Windows

Understanding the core of different operating systems is essential for anyone interacting with computers at a more advanced level. Here's a brief look at three OS families:

- **Unix/Linux:** Known for its robustness and widely used in servers. Popular distributions include Ubuntu, CentOS, and Debian.
- **macOS:** Apple's operating system, built on a Unix-based foundation, combines the power of Unix with a friendly user interface.

- **Windows:** Microsoft's OS, known for its widespread use in personal and enterprise environments.

Example: The command `ls` in Unix/Linux or macOS will list files in a directory. In Windows, the equivalent command is `dir`.

```
cd ~/Projects
ls
file1.txt file2.txt file3.txt
```

Differences Between GUI and CLI

Graphical User Interface (GUI) and Command Line Interface (CLI) are the primary ways to interact with a computer. Understanding the differences can help in choosing the right tool for the task.

- **GUI:** User-friendly, intuitive, and great for beginners.
- **CLI:** Efficient, scriptable, offers more control.

Example: Consider installing a software package. In a GUI, you might click through several menus. In a CLI, a single command can accomplish the same task:

On Linux:

```
apt-get install packagename
```

Using the apt-get command, you can easily install packages on Debian-based Linux distributions.

On macOS, using Homebrew:

```
brew install packagename
```

With the brew command, macOS users can effortlessly install various software packages once they have the Homebrew package manager installed.

Chapter 3

The History of the Command Line

In the initial stages of computer development, graphical interfaces were non-existent, and users communicated with computers solely through text commands. This led to the birth of the command line interface (CLI), an influential instrument that allowed direct interaction with the operating system.

Early Computers

In the 1960s, computer terminals were text-based interfaces without graphical displays. Interacting with these machines required specific commands typed into a terminal. The absence of graphical cues meant users needed to understand the exact syntax and structure of these commands.

Birth of the Shell

The real transformation began with the creation of the first command-line shell. A shell acts as an intermediary between the user and the operating system, translating human-readable commands into something the computer can understand. This made the command line more accessible and versatile.

Evolution of the Command Line

Over time, the command line has evolved, mirroring the development of operating systems and programming languages.

UNIX and the Bourne Shell

```
                                  Terminal
-rwxr-xr-x 1 bin    18296 Jun  8  1979 fsck
-rwxr-xr-x 1 bin     1458 Jun  8  1979 getty
-rw-r--r-- 1 root      49 Jun  8  1979 group
-rwxr-xr-x 1 bin     2482 Jun  8  1979 init
-rwxr-xr-x 1 bin     8484 Jun  8  1979 mkfs
-rwxr-xr-x 1 bin     3642 Jun  8  1979 mknod
-rwxr-xr-x 1 bin     3976 Jun  8  1979 mount
-rw-r--r-- 1 root     141 Jun  8  1979 passwd
-rw-r--r-- 1 bin      366 Jun  8  1979 rc
-rw-r--r-- 1 bin      266 Jun  8  1979 ttys
-rwxr-xr-x 1 bin     3794 Jun  8  1979 umount
-rwxr-xr-x 1 bin      634 Jun  8  1979 update
-rw-r--r-- 1 bin       40 Sep 22 05:49 utmp
-rwxr-xr-x 1 root    4520 Jun  8  1979 wall
# ls -l /*unix*
-rwxr-xr-x 1 sys    53302 Jun  8  1979 /hphtunix
-rwxr-xr-x 1 sys    52850 Jun  8  1979 /hptmunix
-rwxr-xr-x 1 root   50990 Jun  8  1979 /rkunix
-rwxr-xr-x 1 root   51982 Jun  8  1979 /rl2unix
-rwxr-xr-x 1 sys    51790 Jun  8  1979 /rphtunix
-rwxr-xr-x 1 sys    51274 Jun  8  1979 /rptmunix
# ls -l /bin/sh
-rwxr-xr-x 1 bin    17310 Jun  8  1979 /bin/sh
#
```

In 1979, the Bourne Shell was introduced as a part of the UNIX operating system. Its creation marked a significant step in making the command line a standardized part of computing. UNIX's influence can still be seen today in modern OS like Linux and macOS.

MS-DOS and Windows Command Prompt

Parallel to UNIX, Microsoft introduced MS-DOS, with its command-line interface, in the early 1980s. This laid the foundation for the Windows Command Prompt, which many Windows users are familiar with today.

Command Line Today

Despite the advent of advanced graphical user interfaces, the command line continues to thrive in contemporary computing. For certain tasks, it offers a level of efficiency and precision that graphical interfaces cannot match.

The command line remains a fundamental component of many operating systems, providing a powerful tool for software development, system administration, and data analysis. For example, it's often faster to perform complex file operations using a single command line command than navigating through a graphical interface.

Many software applications offer command-line interfaces (CLIs) with advanced functionalities that allow for automation and scripting. Users can perform repetitive tasks quickly and efficiently, particularly in software development and data science, where data processing and model training can be automated.

In the field of cybersecurity, the command line is also an indispensable tool. Cybersecurity professionals use command-line interfaces for tasks such as network monitoring, penetration testing, and digital forensics.

Furthermore, in the world of cloud computing, where virtual machines and servers operate in remote data centres, the command line is often the primary method of interaction. The ability to securely log into remote systems and perform tasks using the command line is a critical skill in managing and maintaining these cloud environments.

In education, the command line continues to be a fundamental part of computer science and IT curricula. Understanding the command line helps students gain a deeper understanding of how computers and operating systems work.

Overall, despite its age, the command line continues to be a relevant and powerful tool in today's computing landscape. Its combination of efficiency, flexibility, and broad application across various fields ensures its continued usage and importance in the foreseeable future.

Modern Shells

Modern shells like Bash, Zsh, and PowerShell offer advanced features, making them vital tools for developers, system administrators, and tech enthusiasts.

The Command Line's Role in Development and System Administration

DevOps and cloud computing have made the command line an essential tool for automation and efficiency in modern technology.

Real-World Impact

Case Studies

- **UNIX Philosophy:** The "Do One Thing and Do It Well" mantra has shaped software design principles.
- **Open Source Movement:** Command-line tools have played a significant role in open-source projects, empowering communities to create and share.

In the Movies

The command line's text-based interface is often portrayed un-realistically in movies as a magical tool used by hackers to break into high-security systems within seconds.

The Hacker Image

In numerous films, hackers are shown rapidly typing away on a command line interface, with streams of text flowing across their screens. This portrayal contributes to the mystique of the "super-hacker" who can infiltrate any system with just a few keystrokes.

Dramatic Real-time Tracking

Movies show real-time tracking of a target on the command line, often accompanied by a map. While command lines can execute various tasks, real-time geolocation in the manner depicted in films is an exaggeration.

Decrypting Passwords

Movie scenes often show characters decrypting passwords instantly using the command line, but in reality, the process is slower and more complex due to password-cracking tools.

Mainstream Movies that Popularized the Command Line

- **"WarGames" (1983):** One of the earliest films to showcase the command line, where a young man accidentally hacks into a U.S. military supercomputer.
- **"The Matrix" Trilogy (1999-2003):** The iconic green command line code became synonymous with the series.
- **"Mr Robot" TV Series (2015-2019):** An accurate portrayal of hacking, with the protagonist often using the command line for various tasks.

Relevance and Impact

While often exaggerated for dramatic effect, the portrayal of the command line in movies underscores its perceived power and importance in computing. These representations have played a role in sparking interest in computer science and cybersecurity for many individuals.

It's important to understand the distinction between the Hollywood version of the command line and its real-world application. Still, the allure and mystique of the command line, as showcased in films, continue to inspire and captivate audiences worldwide.

Chapter 4

Getting Started with the Command Line

Opening the Terminal

Starting with the basics, users must understand how to open the terminal:

- **Terminal in macOS and Linux:** Found in utilities or accessed through keyboard shortcuts.
- **Command Prompt/Powershell in Windows:** Accessed via search or specific keyboard commands.

Real-World Example: A beginner learning how to open the terminal to run a Python script, showcasing that even simple programming tasks often rely on command-line access.

```
# Assume that the Python script is saved in a directory
named 'myScripts' in the user's home directory.
# First, navigate to that directory using the 'cd' (change
directory) command:

cd ~/myScripts

# Once you are in the correct directory, you can confirm
that by listing the contents of the directory:

ls

# If the 'hello.py' file is in the directory, you should
see it listed as a result of the 'ls' command.
# Now, to run the Python script, use:

python3 hello.py

# This command tells Python to interpret your script and
should result in the message "Hello, World!" being printed
to the terminal.
```

In this example, `cd`, `ls`, and `python3` are commands; `~/myScripts` and `hello.py` are arguments to the `cd` and `python3` commands respectively. Note that `~/myScripts` represents a directory path, where ~ is a shortcut for the user's home directory, and `myScripts` is a subdirectory within the home directory.

Understanding the Shell: Bash, Zsh, Powershell

The shell is the user's gateway to the command line:

- **Bash:** A popular shell for Linux and macOS, known for its flexibility.
- **Zsh:** An extended version of Bash with added features.
- **Powershell:** Windows' powerful shell, capable of handling complex system administration.

In these shells, you might want to use a for loop to process a set of files in a directory:

In Bash/Zsh:

```
for file in *.txt
do
  echo "Processing $file"
done
```

In PowerShell:

```
foreach ($file in Get-ChildItem *.txt) {
  Write-Host "Processing $file"
}
```

Command Line Syntax: command, options, arguments

Understanding the syntax is essential for crafting commands:

- **Command:** The action to be performed (e.g., `ls` to list files).
- **Options:** Modifiers that change the command's behaviour (e.g., `-1` for a long listing).
- **Arguments:** The targets of the command (e.g., a specific directory).

Real-World Example: An IT professional using specific syntax to manage user permissions, demonstrating the precision required in many technical tasks.

For example, to change the permissions of a file to read, write, and execute for the owner, read and execute for the group, and only read for others, you would use:

```
chmod 754 myfile.txt
```

In this example, `chmod` is the command, `754` is an option that sets the permissions, and `myfile.txt` is the argument, specifying which file to modify.

Popular Terminal Alternatives: iTerm2, Terminator, and More

While the default terminals on most operating systems are powerful in their own right, many users opt for third-party terminals that offer additional features and customization options. Here are some popular alternatives:

- **iTerm2 (macOS):** iTerm2 is a replacement for Terminal and the successor to iTerm. It offers features like split panes, hotkey windows, and extensive customization options.

  Real-World Example: A developer might use iTerm2's split panes to run a local server in one pane and monitor logs in another, allowing for efficient multitasking without switching between windows.

- **Terminator (Linux):** Terminator provides the ability to arrange multiple terminals in a grid. This can be invaluable for tasks that involve monitoring multiple machines or logs simultaneously.

Real-World Example: A system administrator managing multiple remote servers might have different SSH sessions open in various panes of Terminator, allowing for simultaneous management and monitoring.

- **Hyper (Cross-Platform):** A modern terminal built on web technologies. It's highly extensible and customizable thanks to its use of HTML/CSS/JS. Being cross-platform, it can be used on macOS, Windows, and Linux.

  Real-World Example: A developer who frequently switches between different operating systems might choose Hyper for a consistent terminal experience across all platforms.

- **Alacritty (Cross-Platform):** Touted as the "fastest terminal emulator in existence", Alacritty is a simple yet efficient terminal. It doesn't have tabs or splits, but its speed is unmatched due to its GPU rendering.

All these terminals are extensible and customizable, which is a significant draw for power users and developers. They allow for theming, which can adjust the aesthetics to the user's preference, and many of them support plugins or extensions that can add even more functionality.

By choosing the right terminal emulator, users can tailor their command-line experience to their needs, ensuring maximum efficiency and comfort during extended use.

Chapter 5

Basic Commands

Navigation: cd, ls, pwd

Mastering navigation commands is essential for moving through the file system:

- **cd:** Change directory.
- **ls:** List files and directories.
- **pwd:** Print working directory.

Real-World Example: A web developer navigating to various project folders would use these commands as follows:

```
# Navigate to the main project folder:
cd ~/Projects/MyWebApp

# List files and directories within the current folder:
ls

# Confirm the current directory path:
pwd
```

File Operations: cp, mv, rm, touch

Managing files efficiently is a key skill:

- **cp:** Copy files or directories.
- **mv:** Move or rename files.
- **rm:** Remove files.
- **touch:** Create an empty file.

Real-World Example: Consider an IT professional organizing their files. Here's how they'd use these commands:

```
# Create a new empty file named "notes.txt":
touch notes.txt

# Copy "notes.txt" to the "backup" directory:
cp notes.txt backup/

# Rename "notes.txt" to "meeting-notes.txt":
mv notes.txt meeting-notes.txt

# Delete a file named "old-notes.txt":
rm old-notes.txt
```

Viewing and Editing Files: cat, more, less, nano, vim

Viewing and editing files directly from the command line can save time:

- **cat, more, less:** Display file contents.
- **nano, vim:** Text editors within the command line.

Real-World Example: A system administrator editing configuration files might follow these steps:

These commands illustrate the flexibility and power of the command line, allowing professionals to perform complex tasks efficiently.

```
# Display the contents of a configuration file:
cat config.txt

# Open a configuration file in Vim for editing:
vim config.txt

# View a longer file page-by-page using 'less':
less long-config.txt

# Quickly edit a file using the 'nano' editor:
nano quick-notes.txt
```

Chapter 6

Intermediate Commands

File Permissions: chmod, chown, chgrp

Properly managing file permissions is crucial for security and collaboration:

- **chmod:** Change the permissions of a file or directory.
- **chown:** Change the owner of a file.
- **chgrp:** Change the group associated with a file.

Real-World Example: A team collaborating on a shared code-base might use the following commands to control permissions:

```
# Grant execute permissions to a script for the user:
chmod u+x script.sh

# Change the owner of "data.txt" to "john":
chown john data.txt

# Change the group of "data.txt" to "developers":
chgrp developers data.txt
```

Process Management: top, ps, kill

Understanding and controlling system processes are essential for optimal performance:

- **top:** Display dynamic real-time system statistics.
- **ps:** Snapshot of current processes.
- **kill:** Terminate processes.

Real-World Example: On a server, a system administrator might need to check running processes and terminate a non-responsive application:

```
# View active processes:
top

# Display current processes for a user named "john":
ps -u john

# Terminate a process with a specific PID (e.g., 1234):
kill 1234
```

System Information: df, du, free, uname

Monitoring system resources helps in troubleshooting and op-
timization:

- **df:** Report filesystem disk space usage.
- **du:** Estimate file space usage.
- **free:** Display memory usage.
- **uname:** Print system information.

Real-World Example: A system administrator needs to monitor system resources to troubleshoot a performance issue:

```
# Check disk space usage:
df -h

# Get estimated space used by a directory:
du -sh /home/john

# View memory usage:
free -h

# Print OS information:
uname -a
```

Package Management: apt, yum, brew

Efficiently managing software packages can save a lot of time.

- **apt:** Package management for Debian-based systems.
- **yum:** Red Hat's package manager.
- **brew:** macOS's package manager.

Real-World Example: A developer on a Debian-based system needs to install and manage software:

```
# Update package lists for upgrades and new package
installations:
apt update

# Install a new software package (e.g., "git"):
apt install git

# Remove a software package (e.g., "nano"):
apt remove nano
```

Chapter 7

Advanced Commands

Networking: ssh, ping, netstat, nslookup

Understanding networking commands is essential for remote work and network troubleshooting:

- **ssh:** Secure remote login.
- **ping:** Test network connectivity.
- **netstat:** Network connections, routing tables, interface statistics.
- **nslookup:** Query Domain Name System (DNS) to obtain a domain name or IP address.

Real-World Example: If an IT specialist is trying to identify a connectivity problem, they may use:

```
grep -Eo '[A-Za-z0-9._%-]+@[A-Za-z0-9.-]+\.[A-Za-z]{2,4}'
file.txt
```

Archiving and Compression: tar, gzip, zip, unzip

Archiving and compression are vital for managing large files:

- **tar:** Archive files.
- **gzip:** Compress files.
- **zip/unzip:** Package and unpack compressed files.

Real-World Example: Archiving and compressing a directory:

```
cat file.txt | grep "search_term" > output.txt
```

Searching and Sorting: grep, find, sort, uniq

Searching and sorting are indispensable in handling large amounts of data:

- **grep:** Search text using patterns.
- **find:** Search files in a directory hierarchy.
- **sort:** Sort lines of text.
- **uniq:** Report or omit repeated lines.

Real-World Example: Preprocessing raw data by a data scientist:

```
$ command &
$ jobs
$ fg %1
```

Chapter 8

Scripting Basics

_____

Introduction to Bash Scripting

Automating command line tasks through scripting is popular,
especially in Bash

Real-World Example: Automating daily backups:

```
cp -r $SOURCE_DIR $BACKUP_DIR
```

Explanation:

- This script creates a backup by copying (`cp -r`) a directory (`SOURCE_DIR`) to a backup location (`BACKUP_DIR`).
- The `-r` flag ensures that directories and their contents are copied recursively.

Alias: You can create a convenient alias for this script. For instance, if your script is saved as `backup.sh`, you can add the following to your `~/.bashrc` or `~/.bash_profile`:

```
alias backup="bash /path/to/backup.sh"
```

Variables, Loops, Conditional Statements

Understanding these concepts is fundamental for writing effective scripts:

- **Variables:** Store data for processing.
- **Loops:** Repeat actions.
- **Conditional Statements:** Enable decision-making in scripts.

Real-World Example: Monitoring system health:

```
for i in {1..5}
do
    free_memory=$(free -m | awk 'NR==2{print $4}')
    if [ "$free_memory" -lt 200 ]; then
        echo "Warning: Free memory is below 200MB!"
    fi
    sleep 5
done
```

Explanation:

- `for i in {1..5}`: This begins a loop that will run 5 times.
- `free -m`: This command checks memory usage in MB.
- `awk 'NR==2{print $4}'`: This parses the output from `free -m` to get the free memory value.
- `if [ "$free_memory" -lt 200 ]`: This checks if the free memory is less than 200MB.
- `echo "Warning: Free memory is below 200MB!"`: This displays a warning message.
- `sleep 5`: This pauses the script for 5 seconds before it checks again.

Alias: If you save the script as `check_memory.sh`, you can alias it with:

```
alias checkmem="bash /path/to/check_memory.sh"
```

Writing and Executing Scripts

Writing and executing scripts requires proper formatting and permissions:

- **Writing Scripts:** Using text editors like Vim or Nano.
- **Executing Scripts:** Setting execution permissions and running the script.

Real-World Example: Automating the build process:

```
cp -r $SOURCE_FILES $BUILD_DIR
cd $BUILD_DIR
make
```

Explanation:

- `cp -r $SOURCE_FILES $BUILD_DIR`: This copies the source files to a build directory.

- `cd $BUILD_DIR`: This changes the current directory to the build directory.
- `make`: This command compiles and builds applications from source code.

Alias: If you have saved this script as `build_project.sh`, you can create an alias by:

```
alias buildproj="bash /path/to/build_project.sh"
```

Explanation:

- `alias`: This is a command to create a shortcut.
- `backup`: This is the name of the shortcut.
- `bash /path/to/backup.sh`: This is the command that the alias will run.

Remember to always source (`source ~/.bashrc` or `source ~/.bash_profile`) after adding or updating an alias for the changes to take effect.

Chapter 9

Advanced Bash Scripting Techniques

Scripting is more than just automating repetitive tasks. As you delve deeper into Bash scripting, you'll discover it offers a rich set of features akin to many programming languages. This chapter explores some of these advanced techniques, including functions, array operations, file manipulations, and string handling.

Functions in Bash

Functions allow for reusable blocks of code. They can make your scripts more modular and easier to maintain.

```
# Function to calculate disk usage:

disk_usage() {
  du -sh "$1" | cut -f1
}

directory="/home/user"
usage=$(disk_usage "$directory")
echo "Disk usage of $directory: $usage"
```

Working with Arrays

In Bash, arrays can store multiple values in a variable, making it useful for tasks like iterating over sets of items.

```
# Storing and displaying a list of users:

users=("Alice" "Bob" "Charlie")
for user in "${users[@]}"; do
  echo "User: $user"
done
```

Advanced File Operations

Scripts often involve extensive file operations, from searching for specific files to processing their content.

```
# Finding all .log files and archiving them:

find /var/log -name "*.log" -print0 | tar -czvf
logs_archive.tar.gz --null -T -
```

String Manipulation Techniques

Bash provides powerful tools for string processing, which are especially handy for tasks like parsing log files or manipulating text data.

```
# Extracting the filename from a path:

path="/home/user/documents/file.txt"
filename="${path##*/}"
echo "Filename: $filename"
```

By mastering these advanced techniques, you'll be better

equipped to handle a wider range of tasks and challenges in your Bash scripting adventures. Remember to replace the placeholder URLs with actual ones from Carbon.

Chapter 10

Command Line Prompts for User Input

Introduction to User Input

Getting input from users is essential for many scripts. Bash offers straightforward and efficient methods to interact with users, making scripts more dynamic and engaging.

Basic Input with `read` Command

The Bash command `read` acquires input from the user, reading a single line from standard input (usually the keyboard) by default.

Example:

```
# Prompting user for their name:

echo "What's your name?"
read name
echo "Hello, $name!"
```

Explanation:

- `echo`: This command is used to display messages or output data. Here, it prompts the user with the question "What's your name?".
- `read name`: This command reads the user's input and stores it in the variable `name`.
- `$name`: Variables in Bash are referenced with a $ preceding their name. Here, `$name` retrieves the value stored in the `name` variable.

Using Prompts with `read`

The `read` command can also present a prompt to the user, making the interaction more transparent.

Example:

```
# Using prompt with read:

read -p "Enter your age: " age
echo "You are $age years old."
```

Explanation:

- read -p "Enter your age: " age: The -p option allows read to display a prompt to the user before reading the input. Here, the prompt is "Enter your age:", and the input is stored in the age variable.

Reading Silent Input

For sensitive data, such as passwords, the read command offers a -s option, ensuring that user input remains hidden.

Example:

```
# Reading silent input:

read -sp "Enter your password: " password
echo
echo "Password stored securely."
```

Explanation:

- `read -sp "Enter your password: " password`: The `-s` option hides the user's input, making it suitable for entering sensitive information. The `-p` option then provides a prompt, and the input is stored in the `password` variable.
- `echo`: An empty `echo` command produces a new line, providing a gap before the next output.

Summary

Prompting for user input in Bash scripts creates an interactive experience that can be adapted to various scenarios. The `read` command seamlessly integrates user interaction, whether it's gathering basic data, passwords or multiple entries. Always handle sensitive information, such as passwords, with care and store them securely to ensure safety.

Chapter 11

Bash Scripting Examples

In the evolving realm of technology, automation stands out as one of the key elements driving efficiency. Using scripts, even the most repetitive tasks can be automated, saving time and preventing errors. From simple data backups to intricate server setups, scripting offers unparalleled benefits.

In this chapter, we delve deep into a selection of essential scripts that cater to a range of needs, from the most basic to more advanced. Alongside each script, you will find a comprehensive breakdown, ensuring even the uninitiated can grasp the mechanics at play.

Simple Directory Backup

Backing up data is a practice as old as computing itself. This script provides a straightforward way to create a backup of any directory.

```
cp -r $SOURCE_DIR $BACKUP_DIR
```

Explanation

- cp: This is the copy command in Unix/Linux systems.
- -r: The flag to recursively copy directories and their content.
- $SOURCE_DIR: The directory you want to back up.
- $BACKUP_DIR: The location where you want the backup to be stored.

Alias

For frequent backups, consider crafting an alias. If your script is named backup.sh, append the following to your ~/.bashrc or ~/.bash_profile:

```
alias makebackup='./backup.sh'
```

With this, simply typing makebackup in your terminal would initiate the script.

Batch Rename Files

Renaming multiple files at once can be a daunting task, but with a simple script, the process becomes a breeze.

```
for file in *.jpg; do mv "$file" "prefix_$file"; done
```

Explanation:

- This script cycles through all `.jpg` files in the current directory.
- `mv`: The command used to move or rename files.

- The script renames each file by adding a "prefix_" before the original filename.

Tip: Change *.jpg to another file extension as needed or drop the extension altogether to target all files.

System Uptime Alert

For those running critical systems or servers, knowing your system's uptime can be crucial. This script sends an alert if the system uptime exceeds a set threshold.

```javascript
const pluckDeep = key => obj =>
key.split('.').reduce((accum, key) => accum[key], obj)

const compose = (...fns) => res => fns.reduce((accum, next)
=> next(accum), res)

const unfold = (f, seed) => {
  const go = (f, seed, acc) => {
    const res = f(seed)
    return res ? go(f, res[1], acc.concat([res[0]])) : acc
  }
  return go(f, seed, [])
}
```

Explanation:

- The script first fetches the system's uptime in hours.
- If the uptime surpasses 24 hours, it sends an email alert to the specified email address.
- You'll need to ensure your system is set up to send emails using the `mail` command.

Tip: Modify the threshold and the email content as per your requirements.

Monitoring Disk Usage

Knowing when your disk is about to fill up can save you from a lot of potential issues. This script will send an alert if disk usage goes beyond a certain percentage.

```
#!/bin/bash
MAX=90
USAGE=$(df / | tail -1 | awk '{print $5}' | sed 's/%//')
if [ $USAGE -gt $MAX ]; then
    notify-send "Disk Alert" "Your root partition is almost
full."
fi
```

Explanation:

- The script uses `df` to get the disk usage of the root directory (/).
- If the usage goes beyond 90%, an alert email is sent.
- Ensure your system is set up to send emails using the `mail` command.

Tip: You can adjust the threshold percentage or monitor a different directory as needed.

Automatically Organising Downloads Folder

Over time, the Downloads folder can become cluttered. This script helps organise files in the Downloads directory by moving them into categorised subdirectories.

```bash
#!/bin/bash
cd ~/Downloads

mkdir -p Images Documents Videos

mv *.jpg *.png *.jpeg Images/
mv *.pdf *.docx *.xlsx Documents/
mv *.mp4 *.mkv Videos/
```

Explanation:

- The script first navigates to the Downloads directory.
- It then creates subdirectories for Images, Documents, and Videos.
- Files are then moved to their respective directories based on their extensions.

Tip: You can further categorise and add more file extensions as per your preference.

———————————————

Simple Web Server

If you quickly need to share files over a network, this script sets up a simple HTTP server using Python.

```bash
#!/bin/bash
python3 -m http.server
```

Explanation:

- This script uses Python's built-in HTTP server module.
- By default, it serves on

port 8000. To access the server, go to `http://localhost:8000` on your web browser.

Tip: Use with caution; don't expose sensitive files or run in untrusted networks.

Automated Backup to External Drive

To ensure data safety, it's crucial to have backups. This script will check if an external drive is mounted and then copy important data to it.

```bash
#!/bin/bash
MOUNTPOINT="/media/my_external_drive"
SOURCE_DIR="/home/user/important_data"
BACKUP_DIR="$MOUNTPOINT/backup"

if mountpoint -q $MOUNTPOINT; then
    cp -r $SOURCE_DIR $BACKUP_DIR
else
    echo "External drive not mounted!"
fi
```

Explanation:

- The script checks if the specified mount point (MOUNTPOINT) is an active mount.
- If the external drive is mounted, it copies the data. Otherwise, it prints an error message.

Tip: Make sure you adjust the MOUNTPOINT and SOURCE_DIR to your specific needs.

_____

Batch Image Resize

Suppose you often work with images and need to resize multiple of them. This script leverages the `convert` command from the ImageMagick suite to resize all JPG files in a directory.

```bash
#!/bin/bash
for img in *.jpg; do
    convert $img -resize 800x800 resized_$img
done
```

Explanation:

- The script loops through all JPG files in the current directory.
- For each image, it resizes it to a maximum of 800x800 pixels (keeping the aspect ratio) and saves it with a "resized_" prefix.

Tip: Ensure ImageMagick is installed, and you can adjust the resolution as needed.

Network Check and Alert

If you have unreliable internet, you might want to get alerted when the internet goes down or comes back up.

```bash
#!/bin/bash
HOST="8.8.8.8"
ping -c 1 $HOST > /dev/null 2>&1

if [ $? -ne 0 ]; then
    notify-send "Internet connection" "Internet seems down!"
else
    notify-send "Internet connection" "Internet is back up!"
fi
```

Explanation:

- The script pings Google's public DNS (8.8.8.8) once.
- Depending on the success of the ping, it sends a desktop notification about the internet's status.

Tip: This can be combined with a cron job to run at regular intervals, keeping you informed about your network status.

Bulk File Rename

If you have a directory full of files that need to be renamed in a specific pattern, this script can do the job.

```bash
#!/bin/bash
a=1
for i in *.jpg; do
    new=$(printf "photo_%04d.jpg" "$a")
    mv -- "$i" "$new"
    let a=a+1
done
```

Explanation:

- This script will rename all `.jpg` files in the current directory to a pattern like `photo_0001.jpg`, `photo_0002.jpg`, and so on.
- The `printf` function formats the number with leading zeros.

Monitor Disk Usage

This script helps in monitoring disk usage, and if the usage exceeds a certain percentage, it sends an alert.

```bash
#!/bin/bash
MAX=90
USAGE=$(df / | tail -1 | awk '{print $5}' | sed 's/%//')
if [ $USAGE -gt $MAX ]; then
    notify-send "Disk Alert" "Your root partition is almost full."
fi
```

Explanation:

- It checks the disk usage of the root partition.
- If the usage is greater than 90%, it will send a desktop notification.

Tip: You can adjust the MAX variable as per your needs.

_____

Auto Shutdown After Download Completion

If you're downloading a large file and want your computer to shut down after the download completes, this script can be helpful.

```bash
#!/bin/bash
while [ "$(pgrep wget)" ]; do
    sleep 60
done
shutdown -h now
```

Explanation:

- The script checks if `wget` (a common command-line downloader) is running.
- Once `wget` completes its task and exits, the script will shut down the computer.

Note: Be cautious with auto-shutdown scripts. Ensure no unsaved works or important tasks are running.

Log IP Changes

If you have a dynamic IP and want to keep track of changes, this script logs your external IP.

```bash
#!/bin/bash
DATE=$(date)
IP=$(curl -s http://ipinfo.io/ip)
echo "$DATE - $IP" >> ip_log.txt
```

Explanation:

- The script fetches the current date and the external IP.
- It then logs this data to a file called `ip_log.txt`.

Tip: You can set this up with a cron job to run at specific intervals.

Batch Convert Images

Converting a batch of images from one format to another can be done efficiently using the `convert` utility from the

`ImageMagick` package.

```bash
#!/bin/bash
for img in *.png; do
    convert "$img" "${img%.png}.jpg"
done
```

Explanation:

- This script converts all PNG images in the current directory to JPEG format.
- `${img%.png}.jpg` extracts the filename without the `.png` extension and appends `.jpg`.

Backup Database

This script is useful for taking backups of your MySQL/MariaDB database.

```
#!/bin/bash
USER="username"
PASSWORD="password"
OUTPUT="/path/to/backup/directory"
mysqldump --user=$USER --password=$PASSWORD --all-databases
> "$OUTPUT/alldb_backup.sql"
```

Explanation:

- This script uses the `mysqldump` utility to take a backup of all databases.
- Ensure you replace the placeholders with your actual database username, password, and desired output path.

Caution: Storing passwords in scripts is not secure. Consider using a configuration file or other safer methods.

_____

Automate System Updates

If you want your system to automatically update at regular intervals, this script can help.

```
#!/bin/bash
apt-get update
apt-get upgrade -y
apt-get autoclean
```

Explanation:

- The script first updates the list of available packages.
- Then it upgrades the installed packages.
- Finally, it cleans up the local repository of retrieved package files that can no longer be downloaded.

Note: This example is for Debian/Ubuntu systems. For other distributions, the package management commands will differ.

Monitor Website Availability

This script checks if a website is up and sends a notification if it's down.

```bash
#!/bin/bash
URL="https://www.example.com"
if ! curl -s --head  --request GET "$URL" | grep "200 OK" >
/dev/null; then
    notify-send "Website Down" "$URL is not responding."
fi
```

Explanation:

- The script uses `curl` to send a GET request to the website.
- It then checks the response headers for a "200 OK" status.
- If the status is not found, it means the website might be down, and it sends a desktop notification.

Tip: You can integrate this script with a cron job to get periodic checks.

Chapter 12

Command Line Text Editors

Nano Basics

Nano is a user-friendly command line text editor, great for beginners:

- **Basic Operations:** Opening, editing, and saving files.
- **Shortcuts:** Utilizing built-in keyboard shortcuts.

Real-World Example: Editing a configuration file in Nano:

```
nano /path/to/config/file.txt
```

Vi/Vim Basics

Vi and Vim are powerful text editors, widely used by experienced users:

- **Modes:** Understanding Normal, Insert, and Visual modes.
- **Commands:** Navigating and manipulating text efficiently.

Real-World Example: Editing a script file using Vim:

```
vim /path/to/script.sh
```

Emacs Basics

Emacs is a highly customizable text editor with a steep learning curve:

- **Keybindings:** Learning essential keyboard shortcuts.
- **Extensions:** Enhancing functionality with add-ons.

Real-World Example: Setting up an integrated development environment (IDE) in Emacs:

```
emacs /path/to/project/main.c
```

Chapter 13

Customising Your Command Line

Aliases and Functions

Aliases and functions enable efficient command line usage:

- **Aliases:** Shortcuts for lengthy commands.
- **Functions:** Customized commands with more function-ality.

Real-World Example: Creating an alias and function for common tasks:

```
alias ll="ls -la"
function extract() { tar -xf $1; }
```

Environment Variables

Environment variables store information that influences the behaviour of software:

- **Setting Variables:** Creating and modifying environment variables.
- **Using Variables:** Accessing variables in scripts and commands.

Real-World Example: Setting and using the PATH environment variable:

```
export PATH="$PATH:/path/to/my/scripts"
echo $PATH
```

Customizing Shell Prompt

Personalizing the shell prompt improves the user experience:

- **Colors and Symbols:** Enhancing readability.
- **Information Display:** Adding information such as user-name, host, and path.

Real-World Example: Customizing the shell prompt to show the current directory:

```
PS1="\u@\h \w$ "
```

Installing and Using Oh-My-Zsh or Oh-My-Powershell

These frameworks offer advanced features for Zsh and Power-shell:

- **Installation:** Installing the framework.
- **Themes and Plugins:** Customizing with themes and plu-gins.

Real-World Example: Installing and setting up Oh-My-Zsh:

```
sh -c "$(curl -fsSL
https://raw.githubusercontent.com/ohmyzsh/ohmyzsh/master/too
ls/install.sh)"
zsh
```

Chapter 14

Advanced Topics

Regular Expressions

Regular expressions provide powerful search and manipulation capabilities:

- **Syntax and Patterns:** Understanding symbols and constructs.
- **Searching and Replacing:** Using `grep`, `sed`, and other tools.

Real-World Example: Using regular expressions to extract email addresses from a text file:

```
grep -Eo '[A-Za-z0-9._%-]+@[A-Za-z0-9.-]+\.[A-Za-z]{2,4}'
file.txt
```

Pipes and Redirection

Pipes and redirection control data flow:

- **Pipes (|):** Connecting commands to pass output and input.
- **Redirection (>, >>, <):** Directing output to files or other commands.

Real-World Example: Using pipes and redirection to search for a word in a file and save the output:

```
cat file.txt | grep "search_term" > output.txt
```

Job Control

Job control manages multiple processes:

- **Background Processes:** Running tasks in the background.
- **Managing Jobs:** Using commands like `bg`, `fg`, and `jobs`.

Real-World Example: Running a process in the background and bringing it back to the foreground:

```
$ command &
$ jobs
$ fg %1
```

Chapter 15

Real-World Scenarios

Automating Tasks with Scripts

Automation is a powerful aspect of the command line:

- **Creating Scripts:** Writing scripts for repetitive tasks.
- **Scheduling Scripts:** Using tools like `cron` for regular execution.

Real-World Example: Using a script to automate nightly backups and scheduling them with `cron`:

```
#!/bin/bash
tar -czf /backup/backup-$(date +%F).tar.gz /data

Scheduling with cron:
0 2 * * * /path/to/backup.sh
```

Debugging Scripts

Debugging ensures scripts to function as intended:

- **Common Errors:** Recognizing and fixing syntax and logical errors.
- **Debugging Tools:** Utilizing `bash -x`, `echo`, and other techniques.

Real-World Example: Debugging a script that calculates the average of numbers:

```
#!/bin/bash
sum=0
count=0
for num in "$@"; do
  sum=((sum + num))
  count=((count + 1))
done
echo "Average: $((sum / count))"

$ bash -x avg_script.sh 1 2 3
```

Command Line for Developers: git, docker commands

Developers rely on command-line tools like Git and Docker:

- **Git:** Version control and collaboration.
- **Docker:** Containerization for consistent development environments.

Real-World Example: Using Git for collaboration and Docker to set up a consistent development environment:

```
# Git
$ git clone https://github.com/user/repo.git
$ git add .
$ git commit -m "Initial commit"
$ git push origin master

# Docker
$ docker pull image_name
$ docker run -d -p 8080:80 image_name
```

Chapter 16

Command Line Fun: Games, Effects, and More

Introduction to Command Line Fun

While the command line is a powerful tool for serious work, it can also be a playground for quirky applications, games, and visual effects. Let's delve into some entertaining things you can do right within the terminal.

Classic Terminal Games

1. **Fortune** - Delivers a pseudo-random quote, proverb, or joke. To play, install it and type `fortune` in the terminal.

2. **Cowsay** - A talking cow will display whatever message you type after the `cowsay` command. For instance:

```
cowsay Hello from the terminal!
```

3. **2048-cli** - The classic 2048 game, but for your terminal. Navigate using your arrow keys to merge tiles.

4. **Nethack** - A classic roguelike dungeon exploration game. Dive into the depths and retrieve the Amulet of Yendor!

Note: Some of these games may need to be installed using a package manager like `apt` for Ubuntu or `brew` for macOS.

Fun Visual Effects

1. **Matrix Effect** - Ever wanted to replicate the green rain from "The Matrix" in your terminal? You can achieve this with the `cmatrix` tool. After installing, type `cmatrix` and watch the magic happen!

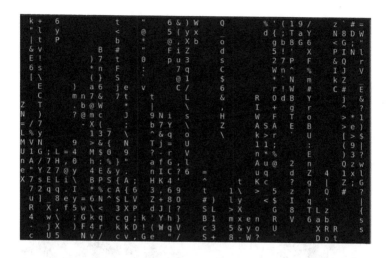

2. **Pipes** - Watch as pipes of random lengths and directions weave and wind across your screen. This can often be seen using the `pipes.sh` script.

3. **Fire Animation** - Simulate a blazing fire in your terminal with `aafire` from the `aalib` package.

Audio in the Terminal

1. **Play Music** - Tools like `cmus` or `moc` allow you to play and manage your music directly from the terminal.

2. **Speak Out** - Use the `say` command (on macOS) to make your computer speak out a phrase:

```
say "Hello, world!"
```

ASCII Art and Animations

1. **Figlet and TOIlet** - These tools turn ordinary text into grand ASCII art banners. For example:

```
figlet Hello!
```

2. **BB** - An ASCII art demo that showcases what can be achieved in the terminal. It includes animations, colours, and even simulated video clips.

Summary

The command line can be both productive and entertaining, with a range of quirky tools and games showcasing the creativity of the developer community. Impress your friends or take a break with these fun terminal tricks!

Note: While most of these tools are available across various operating systems, you may need to check for compatibility or alternative versions tailored for your specific OS.

Chapter 17

Resources for Further Learning

Books

Exploring the command line through books can be beneficial for in-depth knowledge and understanding:

- **Command Line Fundamentals:** Comprehensive guides suitable for both beginners and intermediates.
    - "The Linux Command Line" by William E. Shotts Jr.
    - "Unix and Linux System Administration Handbook" by Evi Nemeth

- **Advanced Topics:** Dive deeper into specific tools and techniques.

- "Mastering Regular Expressions" by Jeffrey E.F. Friedl
- "Pro Bash Programming: Scripting the GNU/Linux Shell" by Jayant Varma

Online Courses

Digital platforms offer interactive courses tailored to different learning paces:

- **Interactive Learning:** Engage in hands-on learning with platforms like Codecademy or Udemy.
    - Codecademy's "Learn the Command Line"
    - Udemy's Unleashing the Mac OS X Terminal for Absolute Beginners (https://www.udemy.com/share/101ODP/)

- **Certifications:** Enhance credibility and skills through certifications like Linux Professional Institute Certification (LPIC) or CompTIA Linux+.

Websites

Websites offer real-time solutions, community support, and up-to-date tutorials:

- **Forums and Communities:** Collaborate, ask questions, and get support on platforms like Stack Overflow or Unix & Linux Stack Exchange.

- **Tutorials and Guides:** Extract knowledge from specialized resources such as 24hoursintheterminal.com, providing real-world scenarios and practical insights.

Chapter 18

Appendix

Common Command Line Shortcuts

Enhancing efficiency in the command line can be achieved through the use of shortcuts.

- **Navigation Shortcuts:** Navigating text swiftly.
    - `Ctrl-A`: Move to the beginning of the line.
    - `Ctrl-E`: Move to the end of the line.
    - `Ctrl-U`: Delete from the cursor to the beginning of the line.
- **Editing Shortcuts:** Modifying command inputs seamlessly.

- `Ctrl-K`: Delete from the cursor to the end of the line.
- `Ctrl-W`: Delete the word before the cursor.
- `Ctrl-L`: Clear the terminal screen.

Troubleshooting Common Issues

Efficiently addressing issues is essential for a smooth command-line experience.

- **Permission Errors:** Encountering "Permission Denied" messages.
  - Cause: Trying to execute, read, or write to a file without appropriate permissions.
  - Solution: Use `chmod` to modify file permissions, or execute commands with elevated privileges using `sudo`.

- **Syntax Errors:** Common mistakes when writing scripts or commands.
  - Cause: Typos, missing symbols, or incorrect command structure.
  - Solution: Review the script or command, check for balanced brackets, and ensure correct syntax.

Glossary of Terms

Dive into the essence of technical jargon for enhanced understanding:

- **Alias:** A shortcut set up in the command line to repre-
  sent a command or sequence of commands, streamlin-
  ing repetitive tasks and simplifying complex command
  sequences.

- **Bash:** A popular Unix shell and command language,
  known for its versatility. It's the default shell for many
  Linux distributions.

- **Command Line Interface (CLI):** A text-based interface used for interacting with software or computer
  programs.

- **Cron:** A Unix-based tool that allows users to execute
  scripts or commands at scheduled times automatically.

- **Daemon:** A background process or program that runs
  continuously, often started during the system booting
  process.

- **Environment Variables:** Dynamic values loaded into the

shell or other running processes. These can influence program behaviour.

- **File Permissions:** Settings that determine who can read, write, or execute a file, are managed using commands like `chmod` and `chown`.

- **GNU:** An operating system and extensive collection of free software. It stands for GNU's Not Unix – a recursive acronym.

- **Kernel:** The core component of an operating system, responsible for resource allocation, file management, and system security.

- **Pipeline:** A sequence of processes chained by their standard streams, ensuring the output of one process is the input of another. It's represented by the pipe symbol (|).

- **Process:** An instance of a computer program being executed, consisting of program code and current activity, is called a process.

- **Regular Expression (Regex):** A powerful tool represented by a sequence of characters. It defines a search pattern, predominantly used by string-searching algorithms for "find" or "find and replace" operations.

- **Shell:** A user interface for accessing an operating system's services. It can be command-line based or have a graphical interface.

- **Terminal:** A tool or environment where users input commands and receive outputs, interacting with a shell.

Chapter 19

Conclusion

The command line is a powerful tool that transcends the boundaries of operating systems and professional roles. Whether you're a beginner interested in basic navigation or an advanced user looking to automate complex tasks, the command line offers endless possibilities.

This book has provided:

- **Fundamental Concepts:** From simple commands to understanding the shell.
- **Intermediate Techniques:** Including file permissions, process management, and more.
- **Advanced Insights:** Networking, scripting, and customization.

- **Real-World Examples:** Practical applications, including insights from 24hoursintheterminal.com.

Your journey doesn't end here. The world of the command line is vast and ever-evolving. Continue to explore, experiment, and learn. The command line is not just a tool; it's a craft that, when mastered, can transform your relationship with technology.

Thank you for embarking on this journey through the command line. May your curiosity continue to drive you forward, and may the command line be a steadfast ally in all your technological endeavours.